How to Play Pipa, the Chinese Lute

– the Basic Skills

H.H. Lee

A guide to playing pipa, the Chinese lute at home by yourself

How to Play Pipa, the Chinese Lute – the Basic Skills

ISBN: 9781549958397

First published on 24 October 2017

Edition 1.2 on 4 October 2019

Table of Contents

Preface

The pipa/琵琶, literally meaning "plucking forward and backward", is a four-stringed Chinese musical instrument that can date back to the Qin Dynasty (221 to 206 BC); yet before the Tang Dynasty (AD 618 to 907), the word "pipa" itself could refer to all kinds of plucked chordophones. Also known as the Chinese lute in the West, the pipa belongs to the plucking family[1] in the modern Chinese orchestra[2].

<u>The pipa and other members of the plucking family</u>

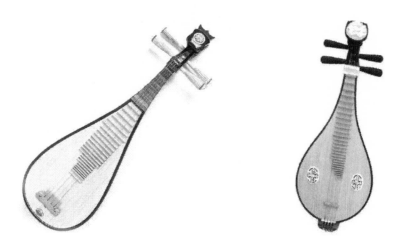

Pipa/琵琶 (left) and Liuqin/柳琴 (right)

---

[1] The plucking family mainly consists of pipa/琵琶, liuqin/柳琴, ruans/阮 (soprano, alto, tenor and bass), sanxian/三弦, guzheng/古筝 and yangqin/揚琴.

[2] The modern Chinese orchestra consists of four families, namely the bowing (bowed string), the plucking (plucked string), the blowing (wind) and the hitting (percussion).

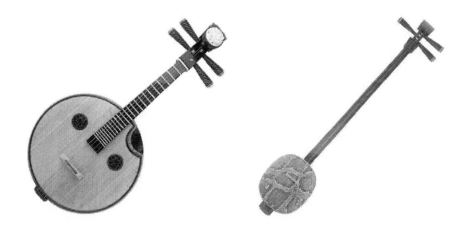

Ruan/阮 (left) and Sanxian/三弦 (right)

The modern pipa evolves from the crooked-necked lute originating in central Asia around the 5th to 6th centuries AD, which bore a resemblance to the Persian *barbat* or the Arabian *ud*. In early times, performers played the pipas with a pick made of bone or wood, but soon they used fingers instead for the sake of agility and dexterity. Since the Tang Dynasty, the pipa has become popular and ranked principally among members of the plucking family, irrespective of playing solo or ensemble. The abundance of overtones, as well as the strong and penetrating timbre, account for the popularity of the pipa throughout the history.

In the following, I will show you how to play the pipa. Even if you are an amateur of Chinese music, you can still play some simple songs with enough efforts. Remember, practice makes perfect! But the first thing to do, doubtlessly, is to choose a pipa.

The Structure of the Pipa

I will illustrate the pipa structure with a 24-fret pipa as shown below:

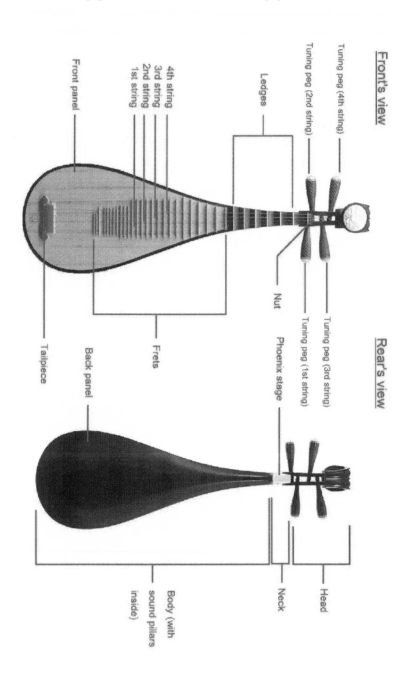

5

The above picture shows the front and rear views of the pipa, which comprises three main parts: the head, neck and body, on which smaller parts including the tuning pegs, nut, phoenix stage, ledges, frets, strings, tailpiece, front panel and back panel can be found (the sounds pillars are built within the body and invisible in this diagram). Their names and respective functions are described as follows:

Name	Description
Head	The head holds the tuning pegs. Carved as a dragon head or phoenix tail in the past, it usually takes the form of a square *ruyi*[3]/如意 nowadays with the aim of beautifying the instrument.
Tuning pegs	The four tuning pegs, with two on each side, are used to vary the tension on the four strings to adjust the pitches (the higher the tension, the higher the pitch).
Nut	The nut is a piece of wood protruding on the head, which marks the starting point of the open strings and defines the vibrating lengths (scale lengths).
Neck	Being the smallest part among all on the body, the neck connects the nut and ledges.
Phoenix stage	The phoenix stage is embedded on the back of the neck for the sole purpose of decoration.
Ledges	The ledges are long triangular pieces of ivory, bone, jade, cow horn or hard wood, with their cross-section as an equilateral triangle. There are altogether 6 ledges (4 in the past), and each of them is given an ordinal number (first to sixth) to

---

[3] The *ruyi* is a kind of curved decorative object that carries an auspicious meaning in Chinese culture.

	indicate their order from top to bottom. Except the 1st ledge, the other five ledges are arranged on the principle of equal temperament, such that each of them is separated by a semitone.
Frets	The frets were absent in crooked-necked lutes, and only came into existence after the Song Dynasty. The number of frets was initially 10, 12 or 13, but has increased to 18, 24, 25 or 28 today. They are long triangular pieces of bamboo, with their cross-section as a trapezium. Likewise, an ordinal number (first to twenty-fourth in our model) was given to indicate their order from top to bottom. The frets are also arranged on the principle of equal temperament, such that each of them is separated by a semitone.
Strings	The four strings of the pipa are named the *chan*/纏 (4th), *lao*/老 (3rd), *zhong*/中 (2nd) and *zi*/子 (1st) strings in Chinese, which are usually tuned at A2, D3, E3 and A3 (this setting of tunes is called the *zhengdiao*/正調) from left to right in the eye of the audience. The current trend is to use pure steel for the *zi* string and nylon-wrapped steel for the other three strings.
Tailpiece (bridge)	The tailpiece is a wooden device embellished with some patterns and fixed on the front panel. Its upper part has four holes through which the four strings are anchored to the body. Besides, it is the ending point of the open strings and defines the vibrating lengths (scale lengths).

Front panel	The pear-shaped front panel, onto which the frets are affixed, is the most important part of the pipa since it determines the volume and quality of the sound generated. Sounds are emitted through a rectangular hole on the front panel, which is beneath the center of the tailpiece.
Back panel	The back panel connects the head at the top and the front panel at the bottom, and forms the resonance chamber with the front panel.
Sound pillars	The sound pillars within the body of the pipa join the front and back panels to construct a hollow chamber for resonance.

After understanding the pipa structure, we now have enough knowledge to choose a pipa for ourselves.

How to Choose a Pipa

The materials used, craftsmanship and timbre determine the quality of a pipa.   As the pipa are made of different materials, we shall look into them one by one:

<u>The back panel</u>

The back panel makes up the main body of a pipa, so its material plays a key role in the overall quality of the pipa.

Same as other wooden musical instruments, amboyna wood is ranked as the best (and of course the most expensive) material for making a pipa. Among them, the red sandalwood (*Pterocarpus santalinus*) has the highest quality and price.   However, given the rarity and for environmental sake, we can also seek the next best redwood, whose quality becomes better on aging.   Old redwood (with an age more than hundreds of years) appears to be dark red in color, whereas new redwood appears to be light red in color.   Rosewood pipas are also acceptable in view of its moderate timbre and price, while the cheapest pipas are made of whitewood and poorest in sound.

The left picture shows a back panel made of the red sandalwood, renowned for its fine texture, gorgeous color, beautiful patterns with comparable durability and resistance to corrosion.

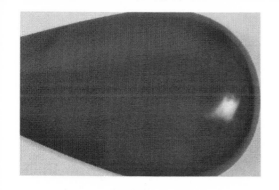 The left picture shows a back panel made of the new redwood (its age can be told from its bright color), which is a commonplace in the market, owing to its lower price and mediocre quality.

To identify the wood species, we can scrape off the paint behind the nut to examine its wood grain and color. If you cannot tell the kind of wood by yourself, it is advisable to ask an experienced person to choose on behalf of you.

The back panel should be ideally made of one single piece of wood, for those formed by several pieces of wood may crack at where they are glued and affect the sound generated when time passes.

The front panel

The front panel make ups the other half of the main body of a pipa, on which the ledges, frets and strings are attached, so it is also vital to the timbre of the pipa.

Chinese parasol trees are good materials for making the front panel, in particular those growing in Lankao County, Henan Province, China. Of course, it is hard to tell the place of origin with naked eyes, and therefore we should pay attention to the craftsmanship.

We should choose a front panel without any knots or cracks; and most importantly, there should not be any gaps in the middle of the panel. In other words, the left and right halves of the front panel should look like a pair of mirror images. Other criteria like the internal volume and curvature of the resonance body, sizes and shapes of the sound pillars inside, etc. cannot be observed from the exterior and are thus ignored.

The right picture shows a front panel made of the parasol wood. The vertical lines thereon are equally distributed, and the two halves are almost perfect reflections.

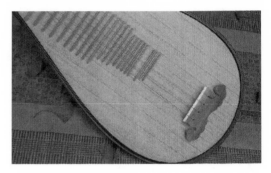

The ledges and the frets

Ledges can be made of ivory or jade, but these expensive materials do not serve better than others save decoration. Actually, redwood is already sufficient for making ledges that can function well. In this connection, the requisite for good ledges is not the material, but rather the craftsmanship – whether they are arranged properly to render the correct notes. For the ledges, we need to check the outer edges of the 1st and 4th strings at the 1st ledge to see whether they are equal in length, otherwise either string will be prone to slip out of the ledge. This defect is mainly attributed to the deviation of the tailpiece from the central axis of the front panel, or the unequally separation of the strings at the nut. Moreover, we have to measure the distance between the upper end of the 18th fret and the strings. The ideal distance should be 0.4 to 0.5 cm by which we can press the strings easily; on the contrary, a distance of more than 0.6 cm will be deemed too much.

The left picture shows the six ledges of a pipa, whereas the circle indicates the 1st ledge. It can be seen that the aforesaid lengths on the two sides (the 4th string to the leftmost edge and the 1st string to the rightmost edge) are not equal, so the ledges are not well made.

The right picture shows the 24 frets of a pipa, whereas the circle indicates the 18th fret. The distance between the strings and the upper end of this fret should ideally be around 0.4 to 0.5 cm to facilitate our pressing of the strings.

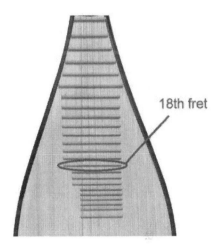

The tailpiece

The tailpiece should be flatted rather than curved, since strings are fastened under normal conditions and will break easily on a curved surface at the upper end of the tailpiece.

A groove is cut into the tailpiece beneath the hole of the 1st string to make replacement of this string easier, because the 1st string breaks more frequently than the others due to its thinness. The groove should have an adequate depth and width (especially the inner side), such that we can really utilize it to change the string.

The right picture shows how the four strings are anchored to the front panel through their respective holes on the tailpiece. We can use the groove indicated by the circle to help replace the 1st string.

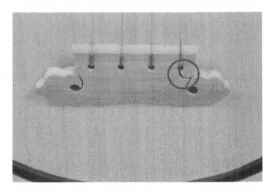

The timbre

Apart from the physical quantities, we also need to listen to the sound generated by a pipa to judge its quality. In fact, a good timbre is the most important criterion among others.

A good timbre encompasses five kinds of sound qualities, including:
1) The brightness of sounds at higher positions of frets;
2) The vigor of sounds at lower positions of ledges;
3) The swiftness of sounds after the strings are plucked;
4) The crispness of sounds at 1st, 2nd and 3rd ledges; and
5) The transmittance of clear sounds over a long distance.

Qualities 1 and 2 cannot coexist with quality 5 on the same pipa, and I personally prefer brightness and vigor to transmittance.

In general, we can choose a pipa that costs less than USD200 for an amateur, which is well painted with tuning pegs and ledges made of cow horn. After several years of practices, we can purchase another pipa of a higher standard, which costs around USD600 and uses Rosewood for the main body, as well as white cow horn for the ledges and tuning pegs.

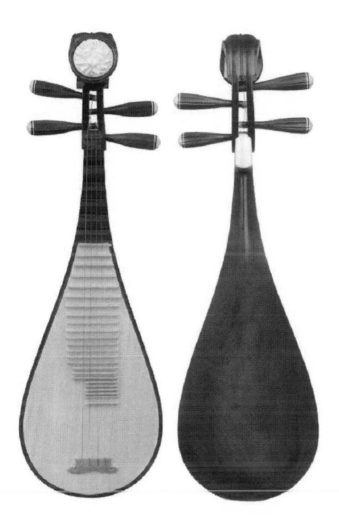

The front and rear views of a common Rosewood pipa available for sale in the market

How to Play the Pipa

Doubtlessly, a correct posture is the prerequisite for playing every musical instrument. When playing the pipa, we have to keep in mind:

The posture

We usually sit on a chair to play the pipa. Choose a chair that is appropriate in height that we can flatten our thighs naturally. Sit still and square our shoulders, chest out and raise our head. Place the pipa between our legs at an angle of 45° against our body. The back panel of the pipa should be a fist away from our chest.

We should remember that the pipa cannot lean on our body, especially the left shoulder, as it will obstruct our left hand's movement.

Hold the pipa in the way shown above

Tuning the strings

Before playing the pipa, we need to tune all of its four strings to ensure that they all produce the correct notes. These notes remain unchanged irrespective of whatever key signatures we refer to, and what actually vary are the solfeggi they represent. To tune the strings, we can make reference to the following table, which depicts all the notes of the pipa:

	4th string	3rd string	2nd string	1st string
Nut	A2	D3	E3	A3
1st ledge	A♯ 2	D♯ 3	F3	A♯ 3
2nd ledge	B2	E3	F♯ 3	B3
3rd ledge	C3	F3	G3	C4
4th ledge	C♯ 3	F♯ 3	G♯ 3	C♯ 4
5th ledge	D3	G3	A3	D4
6th ledge	D♯ 3	G♯ 3	A♯ 3	D♯ 4
1st fret	E3	A3	B3	E4
2nd fret	F3	A♯ 3	C4	F4
3rd fret	F♯ 3	B3	C♯ 4	F♯ 4
4th fret	G3	C4	D4	G4
5th fret	G♯ 3	C♯ 4	D♯ 4	G♯ 4
6th fret	A3	D4	E4	A4
7th fret	A♯ 3	D♯ 4	F4	A♯ 4
8th fret	B3	E4	F♯ 4	B4
9th fret	C4	F4	G4	C5
10th fret	C♯ 4	F♯ 4	G♯ 4	C♯ 5
11th fret	D4	G4	A4	D5
12th fret	D♯ 4	G♯ 4	A♯ 4	D♯ 5
13th fret	E4	A4	B4	E5
14th fret	F4	A♯ 4	C5	F5
15th fret	F♯ 4	B4	C♯ 5	F♯ 5
16th fret	G4	C5	D5	G5
17th fret	G♯ 4	C♯ 5	D♯ 5	G♯ 5
18th fret	A4	D5	E5	A5
19th fret		D♯ 5	F5	A♯ 5
20th fret		E5	F♯ 5	B5
21st fret		F5	G5	C6
22nd fret		F♯ 5	G♯ 5	C♯ 6
23rd fret		G5	A5	D6
24th fret		G♯ 5	A♯ 5	D♯ 6

To tune the pipa, connect the clip-on sensor of a tuner to any string to see whether its open string produces the correct note (A2, D3, E3 and A3 for the four strings respectively); otherwise twist the corresponding tuning peg until the note reaches the right pitch. Repeat this process for all the four strings until the tuning is completed.

The left hand

We press the strings with our left hand. In this respect, our left palm should maintain a certain degree of curvature and stay away from the pipa. Meanwhile, bend our fingers and press the strings slightly above each ledge or fret with the fingertips but not the finger pads.

Bend the fingers in this way to press the strings, as if we were holding a baseball

Use the thumb (but not the junction between it and the index finger) to prop up the neck of the pipa. Relax our forearm and hold our wrist at a proper height. If necessary, adjust our arm in accordance with the change in positions. Don't rest our forearm on the panels, as the muscle will get nervous and it will be difficult for us to press the strings then.

The ways to produce different notes with our left hand will be introduced in the chapter "**The Key Signatures of the Pipa**".

The right hand

We pluck the strings with our right hand. To do so, we need to hold our forearm in a plane parallel to the front panel. Then, grip our right hand as if we were holding something, and bend our wrist inward. According to the shape of the space formed by the thumb and index finger, there are three types of plucking postures:

The dragon-eye typed: The thumb and index finger flex and cross each other to form the shape of a dragon's eye. The thumb, index finger and wrist exert force concurrently. This type produces solid sounds and is suitable for soft and light music.

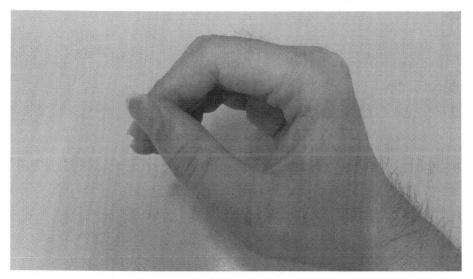

The space encircled by the thumb and index finger resemble a dragon's eye

The phoenix-eye typed: The thumb and index finger extend and cross each other to form the shape of a phoenix's eye. The wrist slightly protrudes and exerts force primarily, whereas the fingers exert force secondarily. This type produces firm sounds and is suitable for strong and fast music.

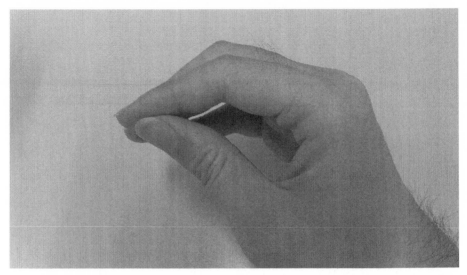

The space encircled by the thumb and index finger resemble a phoenix's eye

The cock-eye typed: The wrist flattens out and the palm relaxes. We only exert force with our fingers. This type produces crisp sounds and is suitable for brisk and energetic music, especially *Jiangnan sizhu*.

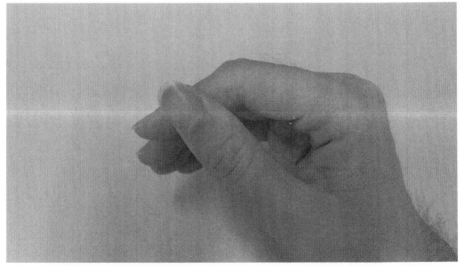

The space encircled by the thumb and index finger resemble a cock's eye

Under all circumstances, our fingers should not stick too close together, in particular our thumb and index finger, which are the mainstay of the plucking motions. We have to relax our wrist as much as possible since anxiety will limit the speed and force in plucking the strings.

After all, let's try to pluck the strings.

We can either strike the strings *leftward* with the right side of the index finger's nail (*tan*) or *rightward* with the left side of the thumb's nail (*tiao*). *Tan* and *tiao* are two fundamental techniques of the right hand.

As for *tan*, first grip the right hand in the dragon-eye shape, and pluck a string leftward by extending the 1st and 2nd joints of the index finger. Our fingers should point at the front panel rather than the left to produce clear and solid sounds. Retrieve our fingers to form the dragon-eye shape again to complete the whole process. *Tiao* is similar to *tan*, save that we extend the joint of our thumb to pick the string. Don't touch other strings inadvertently when retrieving our thumb to restore the previous dragon-eye shape.

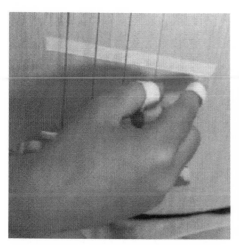 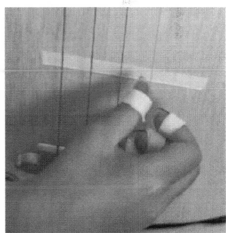

Tan (left) and *tiao* (right) from the audience's viewpoint

Considering that the pipa strings are made of steel, we should wear false nails to protect our own nails when plucking the strings, so as to avoid damage. False nails are usually made of celluloid nitrate, tortoise shell or plastic. They should be moderate in thickness, tough and wearable with a smooth surface, such that they can assist us in plucking the strings for a long period of time.

We can obtain a set of five false nails at a very low price from the Internet

We should choose false nails that are almost identical to our own nails in shape and color except that they are a bit longer. False nails of inappropriate sizes will either be easily detached from our nails, or squeeze and hurt our fingers. False nails can be affixed horizontally (as shown in the right picture) or in a crossed manner by using adhesive plaster or bandage.

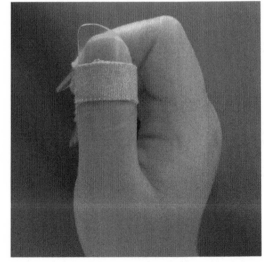

It is more common to affix false nails horizontally with adhesive plaster

Thereafter, we can start playing simple songs, though beforehand we have to learn to read the **numbered musical notation**, which is widely adopted in Chinese sheet music.

The Numbered Music Notation

The excerpt of the sheet music of a Sudanese folk song, *The Hometown Sun*, is attached below for demonstrating how to read and interpret sheet music recorded in the numbered music notation:

The Hometown Sun

Sudanese Folk Song
Arranged by LIU Dehai

The numbered music notation is based on the French Galin-Paris-Chevé system and known as *jianpu*/簡譜 in China. The sheet music for all Chinese musical instruments (including the pipa) is

22

written in this notation, so we must learn to read it.

General principles

The numbered music notation gets its name because it uses numbers (0 – 7) to represent musical notes, but the numbers indeed tally with the solfeggi directly:

1 = do; 2 = re; 3 = mi; 4 = fa; 5 = sol; 6 = la, 7 = si/ti; and 0 = a rest irrespective of the key signatures of the sheet music.

Now let's examine the above sheet music part by part in detail.

1) The name of the song "*The Hometown Sun*" is located at the top;

2) The origin/ (composer/) arranger of the song "*Sudanese Folk Song*" and "*Arranged by LIU Dehai*" are located at the top-right corner;

3) The key signature (1 = D), time signature (2/4) and tempo (♪ = 160) of the song are all located at the top-left corner;

4) The small number inside the bracket indicates the current bar number (the 5th, 10th, 15th, 20th, 25th, 30th, and 35th of this song are marked accordingly, which are all the last bar of every line). The bars are usually arranged in the order of a number's multiple (like there are 5 bars per line in this sheet music), but the actual arrangement depends on the number of notes present within a bar. More notes will lead to fewer bars per line.

5) The following signs carry the same meaning in both staff and numbered music notations:

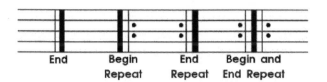

End   Begin   End   Begin and
       Repeat   Repeat End Repeat

For instance, the repeat signs in Bars 21 and 33 signify the single repetition of the phrase in-between, and then jump to Bar 34 and carry on.

The key signature

The key signature is indicated by the expression 1 = X for majors and 6 = X for minors, though the minor notation is never used as far as I have observed.   This song is in D major as indicated by 1 = D.

You may notice the numbers inside the brackets (5   1   2   5), which indicate that the OPEN strings of the four strings (from left to right in the eye of the audience) will produce the solfeggi "sol" (5), "do" (1), "re" (2) and "sol" (5) of the D major respectively.   The relationship between the majors and solfeggi of the open strings will be explained in the next chapter.

The octaves are represented by adding a dot above or below the number. A dot below the number lowers the note by an octave, whereas a dot above the number raises the note by an octave.   For example, i is at an octave higher than 1 whereas 1 is at an octave lower than 1 .

The sharp (♯) sign raises the note by a semi-tone and the flat (♭) sign lowers the note by a semi-tone, whereas the natural (♮) sign neutralizes any sharps or flats from preceding notes or the key signature.

The time signature

The time signature is represented by fractions such as 2/4, 4/4, 6/8…
which mean that there are 2 quarter notes per bar, 4 quarter notes per
bar and 6 eighth notes per bar respectively. In this song, there are 2
quarter notes per bar as indicated by the fraction 2/4.

The tempo

The tempo, if any, will be written next to the time signature in the form
of ♪ = X, which means that there are X quarter notes per minute. In
this song, ♪ = 160 means that there are 160 quarter notes per minute.
Sometimes, you may find a symbol 廿, which means "Ad libitum".
Nonetheless, the tempo will vary as per the requirements of individual
songs.

The note value

Underlined notes (like the solfeggio " 1 " in Bar 10) will have their
lengths decreased by half per underline they have. On the contrary,
notes followed by dots will have their lengths increased by half per dot
they have. If they are followed by a hyphen (like the solfeggio "3 - " in
Bar 23) instead of a dot, their lengths will be doubled.

Though absent in the above sheet music, dynamics (*p, f, mf, mp, ff, pp*),
hairline crescendos and diminuendos will be written below the notes if
necessary.

There are also pipa-specific marks that instruct us how to play the notes
correctly. Musical symbols commonly found in pipa sheet music are

Surviving and Thriving as a Targeted Individual:
How to Beat Covert Surveillance, Gang Stalking, and Harassment

Cathy Meadows M. S., Clinical Psychology

I'm a consultant, advocate, and expert witness for people who are being targeted by covert crimes. The types of crimes that my clients suffer include: being stalked and harassed by groups of people, workplace mobbing, public mobbing, illegal entry into their homes and vehicles, extreme slander, computer and phone hacking, bugging of their homes, phones, etc., constant surveillance, vandalism, biological/chemical assaults, and remote weapons' assaults. Whether the harassment is due to whistleblowing, domestic battles or break-ups, property ownership or wealth, or simple revenge, the reasons that my clients are being targeted can always be traced back to fear, vengeance, or money, and sometimes to all three.

Mind Judo

In order to survive this type of harassment you have to tweak your thought processes and reactions. To begin with, it helps to use a certain amount of thought judo. When people are behaving horrendously towards you, realize that they are sad and suffering themselves. They realize that their actions are wrong but they are unable to stop acting out. It's compulsive and automatic and is symptomatic of someone with a personality disorder, like Sociopathy or Narcissism.

People with personality disorders may share certain traits but the most malignant and dangerous ones are those who have witnessed horrible things in childhood, and I'm not talking about a spanking. Even if they go around screaming, "Mom, God, Country, and Apple Pie" Mom wasn't always that protective or good to them..

Your stalkers are out of control, obviously, but you must not follow suit. You can and should remain in control of your behavior and be an example to them and to others by maintaining an upstanding, fearless, and open persona. They may be living in the darkness of secrecy and fear but you must remain in the light. There you will find health, safety, and sanity.

This is easier said than done because the harassment is constant and unrelenting. However, if you can't find a philosophy or a mind tweak that will allow you to move on without feelings of fear, obsession, and vengeance then you are mirroring your enemy's personality traits. I'm not speaking about anger, either. Righteous anger gets things done, and can change the course of history, just as righteous love does, particularly when they intersect (You can see this intersection clearly in Martin Luther King Jr.'s final speech. The anger is palpable but so is the love.). Therefore, carry on fearlessly with your plans, hopes, and dreams regardless of what's going on in the shadows. Living in the darkness is not a healthy or happy place to be.

Light and Darkness, Good and Evil, Health and Disease

When we speak of someone as living in the darkness or living in the light we are speaking about whether he or she has a negative turn of mind or a positive one. Negative is dark and positive is light. Negative thinking is heavy and cumbersome, but positive thought is light and airy. The fact that stalkers and abusers have to hide what they are doing automatically puts them in the negativity column as that's a lot of weight to carry and over time it takes its toll.

Let me give you an example by way of a few experiments about compassion, and there have been many. When someone shows a kindness to someone else the receiver of the kindness, the giver of the kindness, and everyone watching the kindness gets an immediate boost in their serotonin levels, and in their white blood count. (http://www.medicaldaily.com/random-acts-kindness-sweet-emotion-helping-others-dopamine-levels-383563) A boost in serotonin alleviates mental illness to some extent, and a boost in the white blood count alleviates disease to some extent. Over time, these boosts build up and after 20-30 years of lightness...well, the outcome is obvious.

The opposite can be said for those who harbor ill will towards others. Their serotonin levels and their white blood counts are lower than average. In layman's terms, I think it's nature's way of disposing of dickheads. Too many dickheads can cause evolution and civilization to come to a crashing halt. Now, dickheads will normally counter this argument by saying that they once knew a fellow dickhead and he lived to be 85. This may be true but did he live happily and pain free, and how do they know that? Maybe he could've lived to be 105 and his life was cut short by 30 years. That's a lot of time to lose, unless you're miserable and begging for death.

On the other hand, some people might point to a decent human being who went to an early grave, and had an awful life filled with disease, loneliness, and desperation. Don't forget, the question is whether or not an individual lives in the darkness or in the light, and not whether or not someone is a decent person. An individual's decency won't make any difference to their life expectancy, happiness, or health if they are constantly self-pitying, filled with hopelessness, and are complaining all the time. If their minds are filled with that kind of crap then they are still living in the darkness because they are continuously beating themselves up, which over time affects their health and well-being.

It's no contest. Good guys who live in the light do win in the long run. Though it seems lthat they open themselves up to endangerment while fighting the powers of darkness, it's actually the bad guys who have a better than average chance of going down. A statistic handed down by my Abnormal Psychology teacher to my class in the Master's program is that psychopaths have a better chance of getting murdered then people in the general population. To press the point, people honor and recognize the light. How often do you see landmarks and streets named after good guys, like Lincoln, Martin Luther King, Washington, Jefferson, or Franklin?

Ever hear of a street called Adolf Hitler Boulevard? No, and you never will. The Darkness is dust.

Controlling Your Thoughts and Behaviors (so no one else can)

How can you improve your life, present and future, in the face of relentless attacks? First, you have to realize that's it's going to take work. Recognize that it's an ongoing process that will hold your attention on a regular basis. Your enemies, and/or their emissaries, are using all of their time and energy to bring you down psychologically, physically, financially, and socially. They may be laying awake nights dreaming of your demise. Accept that and move on. Don't get involved in trying to figure out why they're doing what they do.   It's a waste of time. Instead, fill your time walking towards your dreams. If the stalkers make you angry, then let it be righteous anger. You are allowed to express your anger. Put it in a blog, or say it out loud in the privacy of your home without care of who hears it, and then carry on.   By the way, did you know that professional women who drop the F-bomb regularly are psychologically healthier than those who don't? It's healthy to express rage because it's a vehicle for the release of toxins caused by the negativity, and it empowers you.

I'm not going to lie to you. Being stalked, harassed and targeted 24/7 will slow you down. It's a disability to one extent or another but in time it gets better as your positive responses become automatic.. Remember that most averaget Americans believe, at one time or another, that their lives are difficult, even if they aren't being targeted.   People live with all kinds of calamities and disabilities that slow them down. When I feel defeated, cornered, and ruined I think about Stephen Hawking. He has managed to overcome ALS and is paralyzed from top of his head to the tip of his toes, and still continues to write books, make documentaries, do public speaking, and has become one of the most interesting and famous scientists in the world. Stephen Hawking first became afflicted with ALS when he was in college at the age of 25. Since then he has fathered 3 children and has been married twice. Now, what's your excuse again?

Never, ever give up! Ever! That's the end game of what your stalkers hope to accomplish; to make you give up, go sit in a corner, and cower in the dark. Don't do it. Keep walking; walk faster, even, and accomplish everything that you want to accomplish. There are ways to get around things. You can do this and I can help.

Things that you can do to lift your spirits and keep you on the right track.

*Positive affirmations about yourself and your endeavors. Look at yourself in the mirror while doing this.

- Get fresh air and stay on your feel as much as possible. Open up windows and pace while talking on the phone, for example.

- Stay socially active if if you live alone. Call old friends or family on the phone, even if you haven't talked to them for awhile.

- Never complain to anyone about the covert harassment. Many people complain to friends, family, and lovers hoping to find help. Generally, it's rude to dump on your relatives and on the people you love, and chances are they won't believe you anyway. Worse yet, they'll think you're crazy. Talking about this to people is a good way to drive them away and isolate yourself, which is what your enemies want.

- Try not to think about the harassment all day long. Don't obsess about it. Don't continuously run and look out the window, or crawl around trying to figure out where some noise came from, for example. There's nothing your enemies love more then for you to waste all your precious time. Find things to do to occupy yourself besides researching it on the internet 24/7. Obsession leads to insanity so don't go there. Control your own thoughts.

- Do not investigate every little noise you hear in your home. That's obsession. Trying to hear for messages that the ceiling fan is sending to you can be hazardous to your health. If a noise is bothering you, turn off the instrument or put on headphones, or leave. Do other fun things, instead. Play video games, socialize, have sex, flirt, jog, swim, listen to stand-up comedians on youtube, etc.

- If you can't get at least 6 hours sleep at night don't fret. Go and watch the late show and have a snack. Stay up and fall asleep on the couch, if you like. My father use to say that you don't need a lot of sleep. As long as you're in a horizontal position, and your eyes are closed, you'll get enough rest. Fretting about not sleeping is worse for you then not sleeping.

- Stay clean and keep your surroundings clean. Look as good as you can, nearly every day.

- Don't forget to have fun and interesting relationships. Never give up trying to find a lover/friend and someday you might find one, even if you can't get married or live with someone, or even if you have to have serial relationships. You may have to lower the bar with regards to income or attractiveness, but never lower the bar with respect to how you want to be treated.

- Never give up trying to be successful and someday you will be. It may take more time and you'll have to do it while dodging bullets, but you can still do it.

- Do a lot of googling of inspirational quotes about good and evil, love, or simply about life in general. Look up inspirational words from other targets like MLK jr., and Jesus, or find out what the Bible or Buddhism has to say about treachery, deceit, etc. It can carry you through to see how others feel about things.

- Be friendly to everyone, even the bad guys.

- Don't concern yourself with all the hatred aimed at you. Why should you? It's not your sin. Let all of them take their sins to their graves. It's not your problem.

- Love the people who love you. Love them up with hugs, a friendly ear, and little gifts or thoughtful actions. Don't talk about the craziness of the harassment with those you love and with those who love you. All of your time with the people who love you should be dedicated to making them joyful and in return they will make you joyful. When you are with loved ones, consider it that you are taking a break from the war, just like all good warriors do.

Going Down-Alleviating Depression

There are times when you are going to feel sad and under the weather, and you may even get depressed behind the abuse that happens to targets. First of all, don't underestimate the power of simply calling a friend, family member, or acquaintance. It's okay to relate that you are sad and down and need someone to talk to. It's okay to say you are sad because you can't find work, or don't have enough money, or are lonely but try not to talk too much about the methods of harassment being used against you. You can be honest about some negativity in your life but keep it general. You can say that someone is bad-mouthing you for example, or that you are black-balled, but if you get into all of the little abuses targets suffer 24/7, it could ruin the relationship. Sometimes just a few minutes on the phone with someone can brighten your world.

Something else you can do is to go jogging, or simply jog in place at home with the windows open and the music on. We know that exercise releases happy chemicals like endorphins, and it has the added benefit of keeping you in good shape.

Eat chocolate. This really works.

Do something nice for yourself. You know how you never get yourself that special treat because of the calories or the cost? Well, get it anyway and make an occasion out of it, if you like.

Create something whether it be a pot-holder, scarf of a blog going about whatever interests you. Or, work a lot and acquire a lot of money. Whatever makes you happy, go and do it.

Join meetup.com and go to a meeting that interests you so that you can check out new people. It's true that extreme slander is used against targets so make sure you look and feel great when you go out. Look sharp Look groomed and put on some make-up, or small but nice jewelry. It's important to cast yourself in a positive light to turn up your self-esteem, which your enemies are trying to knock down, so dress up, or at least look decent, regularly.

Research for yourself which herbs and foods have antidepressant types of chemicals and effects.

If you get seriously depressed it's wise to at least consider going to a psychiatrist for two reasons. Sometimes just going in to talk to someone about your sadness and getting medication can help, particularly if you're thinking about suicide. Also, if you ever plan to sue your stalkers it helps to show damages, and psychological damages due to criminal harassment, civil rights abuses, and whistleblower retaliation and can and have been used against stalkers and harassers with some success.

Most importantly, act like you're happy even if you're not. Force yourself to smile and laugh all day long. When people ask how you're doing, tell them you're going well. Share funny stories with others. Listen to stand up comedy on iheart.com, and watch stand-up comedians on youtube for free. Look up jokes on the internet, too. Read and watch inspirational and uplifting stories and don't get sucked into someone else's nightmare.

Studies show that just pretending to be happy can have as good an effect as antidepressants have on severely depressed patients. Sometimes better. So suck it up and smile.

Taking Care of Your Temple

It's hard to overstate the importance that simple cleanliness and hygiene has on your physical and emotional health. A clean and orderly environment reflects back at you and helps you to think more clearly. Any movement towards ordering your environment is a good one, even if you don't get to cleaning out the closet right away. Just keep the living environment tidy.

Also, personal hygiene goes a long way towards eliminating discomfort and disease. Shower daily, brush your teeth and clean your mouth before you go to bed and when you wake up, use natural, healing, or fragrant oils on your body, and look good. It can't be over-stated that grooming is important so invest some time into it. If you're a woman use make-up, and if you're a guy tweak that facial, nose, and ear hair. Remember, people are looking at you so present yourself well. Look extra good.

If you are afraid of contracting cancer from all of the targeting you should remove meat from your diet and try to remove animal products from your diet. Even if you can't do this completely, do it as much as you can. It's a fact that vegans have 8 times fewer incidents of cancer then meat eaters (See the movie, What the Health.)

Being targeted takes nutrients out of your body so you should find a good multivitamin and mineral supplement that you can take a couple of times a week. I like Flintstones vitamins for children because they're easily digestible and chewable. It's wise to also take some extra vitamin C, as well. Further, you should eat foods with lots of vitamin A and lycopene like tomato sauce or tomato juice, 3 times a week. Vitamin A and lycopene prevent certain cancers and other diseases like emphysema. Cod liver oil also has vitamin A and other nutrients that are life giving, and Omega-3 Fatty Acids, and b vitamins are necessary for a healthy brain and nervous system.. Lastly, get natural vitamin D by going out in the sun without sunblock for 10-20 minutes a day.

Along with the supplements mentioned earlier, take 3 tablespoons of apple cider vinegar in your food or drink regularly, and use vinegar as a body and scalp rinse, too, a couple of times a week. Use mouthwash during the day, whenever necessary ,and carry a trial size around with you.

As far as your psychological health is concerned, try using Valerian Root for stress and anxiety. You can buy it over-the-counter at any drugstore or department store. Also, chocolate, coffee, and tea are mild anti-depressants. Use them as much as you like. Research natural remedies for your ailments over the internet. There are many things you can try which could work for you.

If you can add these few supplements to your diet, and get some fresh air and sunshine daily, I promise that you will feel and look better.   If you're not taking any supplements now, the difference in how you'll feel within a week or less can be amazing. Taking herbal or vitamin enriched supplements with food 3 times a week is all you really need to cover your needs.

It's interesting to note that people who take antacids live longer. Also, people who take ibuprofen, and other types of anti-inflammatories regularly, live longer. Anti-inflammatories are important for targets because regardless of the type of targeting you're getting hit with, it probably causes inflammation., which in turn causes cancer and other diseases.

Why Are You Being Targeted?

Understanding the reason for your targeting goes a long way towards maintaining a healthy outlook on life in general. Sometimes the reason for the targeting is easy to figure out. For example, if just prior to the targeting you called the cops on someone, blew the whistle on someone, reported wrongdoing to anyone, just got out of an abusive relationship, had intellectual property wiped from your computer, filed a complaint, threatened a lawsuit, witnessed a crime, committed a crime, or you're a political activist, or have money/property that someone else wants to steal, or you're the wrong color or flavor for the neighborhood you're in, that's probably the cause. However, some people can't readily identify the cause for the targeting. Sometimes, it's helps to consult with a professional and just talk it out until you hit on the reason. Sometimes the targeting appears random and there's no apparent reason. In this case the targeting could be because of professional or personal jealousies and competitions that are not being openly expressed by your enemies. There is also the possibility that you might be the victim of experimental research being done on a specific population of persons, or on the public in general.

The truth is that if there is an obvious reason why you're being targeted, it's easier to go forward with a lawsuit or restraining order. If the reason for the targeting is nebulous and hidden, it's much more difficult to prove that the covert harassment is happening and that you're not imagining it. Therefore, it's recommended that you talk to a professional to help you figure out the reason for the targeting, even if the reason is something simple like you just don't fit into your environment.

Types of Targeting

A very large part of the targeting is designed to drive the you into a state of paranoia, or to make you appear to be paranoid, so as to nullify any complaints that you've made, or will make about anything related to the targeting itself.

In order to do this, it's important for the stalkers to destroy the reputation of the target so that others in the environment will allow, take part in, or ignore the criminal harassment and abuse leveled against the target. Accusations against the target are very much over-the-top and efforts to prove that the target is dangerous often extend to exhibiting falsified law- enforcement documents to people in the target's environment.

After the individual has been demonized and made to look paranoid, the more serious abuses against the target's civil and constitutional rights begins, along with attacks on the target's health and well-being. Targeting is a step by step program that is designed to completely destroy the individual in every way imaginable; psychologically, physically, professionally, personally, and financially. It feels like the attacks are personal and sometimes they are, but not always. Not if you're a whistleblower, or an activist, for example.

The majority of targets talk about being stalked, harassed and mobbed publicly, being slandered, having their belongings tampered with or vandalized, being sleep deprived due to noise campaigns, biological/chemical attacks, or remote weapon's attacks in the middle of the night, constant infections and/or pain, 24/7 surveillance, and phone/computer bugging and hacking, These are the most common complaints, There are other complaints and all complaints are taken seriously.

Most targets end up at a doctor's office to get either antibiotics, tooth extractions, anti-anxiety meds, sleep meds, anti-psychotic meds, or medicine for digestive problems. It's smart to visit a doctor when you have to but you could spend all your time at a doctor's office if you don't learn how to care for yourself, to some extent. Google home remedies.

Can The Targeting Be Stopped?

On occasion, I've found that for some the targeting has stopped or has slowed down, at least temporarily, but it's difficult to shut the targeting down completely and forever. Even if you win some kind of a harassment and stalking case in court, the targeting does continue on some level. Targeting people out of fear, for reasons of theft, to save face, or for revenge has become very profitable.   It has become an industry that employs or trades with many different people from many different venues. There are insidious and dangerous businesses that have cropped up to provide targeting services.

I would never dissuade anyone from exploring a legal option to the targeting, and the only reason anyone should pursue a legal route is to bring attention to the problem, because the targeting doesn't probably won't end and could actually get worse. Further, you'd have to have a pretty strong case and be able to present it concisely and objectively if you want to go to court. The stalkers aren't going to make it easy, either. You may want to check out James Walbert's court presentation for cues about how to present a case legally (https://www.youtube.com/watch?v=1xlkLsvziml).

However, if you don't think you can win a case in court then there are other things you can do to try to end the harassment and abuse. Here are the stories about how some of the people I've worked with ended the targeting.

The first story about how to stop gang-stalking and harassment came from an unknown female who called me on the phone one day a few years ago and told me that she had found a way to stop the harassment, and that she's certain it would work for many other targets. She told me that first, she started to volunteer around town including at homeless shelters, soup kitchens, old age homes, etc., and simultaneously began going to church, and began praying while at home. Within 6 months all of the abuse, including the slander, illegal entry, and remote weapons attacks simply ended. Now, she had to volunteer most of her waking hours but it did work.

It's quite understandable that her behavioral change would defuse the gang-stalking and harassment. When you break down the reasons for gang-stalking to basic emotions you can see that the reasons for it have elements of fear within it. This particular target had alleviated some of the fear by doing good deeds, and by appearing non-threatening (going to church). It's much more difficult for stalkers to slander someone who gives unselfishly, and is openly kind to others and expects nothing in return.   Maybe her stalkers came to like her, or maybe they felt powerless to continue but for whatever the reason, this particular target became a lost cause.

On another occasion, a client of mine was able to end the harassment, at least temporarily, by moving to a 3rd world country in South America. Unfortunately, the harassment started up again after a year or two. She was unable to escape the harassment and abuse for the long term, but if she had kept moving around South America maybe she could've. Many targets have successfully stopped their targeting, at least temporarily, by moving around the planet and some have stopped it permanently. However, continuously moving around depletes your bank account and stymies your social and family life. Therefore I don't advise moving around forever unless you're wealthy, and even then you have to make sure that no one is stealing from you over the course of your spending.

More recently, I met someone at a party and I rolled our conversation into the area of gang-stalking and harassment. He knew exactly what I was talking about and told me that the same thing was happening to him until a picture of his father shaking the hand of a congressman appeared on the front page of the newspaper. One of his friends who had come down to California from Oregon for a visit joined the conversation and he was also fully aware of the gang-stalking, etc. They even exchanged some of the ways that they fought back and diverted the stalkers.

Though I am happily surprised to hear of how these people have escaped their gang-stalking, there are times when it appears to be insurmountable. Like when you're talking lawsuits and revenge, you're probably not going to be able to stop it and it might get worse. Also, if it's personal and someone just wants to strongarm you, or is vengeful, jealous, or competitive, it might not stop until the criminal feels like you're out of the way. Likewise, when criminal stalkers and abusers pin all of their hatred of a certain religion, gender, lifestyle, race, or sex, on you, it's probably going to be difficult to escape, simply because the targeting is more about the nasty feelings that the stalker feels then it is about the victim. These stalkers are just looking to vent some of the disgust, horror, or fear in their own hearts and souls and they'll pin that on anyone they can for any reason, or for no reason, in particular.

Without a doubt, there are those who have serious and dangerous personality disorders who have initiated gang-stalking and harassment towards estranged spouses, girlfriends, and significant others, and who have been seriously abused as children. As far as the state of their psyche's go, these types are like serial killers because the abuses they do are only out of vengeance and hatred for some symbol, like a mother figure, for example.

More recently, I was in contact with someone who said that the harassment simply stopped for no apparent reason. This person was suffering with V2K (voice to skull technology) and was experiencing none of the other more commonplace symptoms of gang-stalking and harassment like mobbing, slander, illegal entry, biological/chemical attacks, gas-lighting, etc. This person was very involved with family, work, and associates and rarely malingered. It is advisable to stay busy because hanging around with nothing to do and no one to talk to, and internalizing the harassment, tends to enhance it's effects. There are psychological and sociological reasons for this like, when one's mind is busy there's little room for anything else to squeak through. Also, an isolated target is an easy target so surrounding yourself with as many friends and family as you can is always recommended.

Once, about 10 years ago, a friend of mine said that he knew a few targeted people who went to Greece together for a couple of years and the harassment didn't follow them there. Nor did the harassment start up again when they returned to the USA.

Then there's the target I was in contact with on MySpace around 12 years ago who said that he was only targeted in his hometown where he lived but not when he went to Texas. Go figure. As far as I've heard, this isn't what usually happens, unfortunately. What seems to happen is that the harassment follows the target but it might be a little lighter. However, it's still a good idea to test the theory even if you aren't going to move out of the country permanently.

The most important way to escape the harassment is psychologically and emotionally, however. If you are going forward with your life socially and professionally as much as possible, and you are continuing to be active and hopeful for your future, then you have won the game and we can safely say that you have disabled the machine. Let's not forget that the whole existence for gang-stalking, covert surveillance, and harassment is for mind control. If your enemies can't influence you to give up on your hopes and dreams, or to act out negatively, then the program is a waste of time, energy, and money for everyone involved and should be abandoned immediately. If not, you just keep winning by staying involved in being successful, however you define success. Always hope. Hope is the beginning of miracles, literally.

Think Back to the Days When...

Do you remember what it was like before the targeting or before you knew it was happening? Do you remember where you were working, who you were dating, and your general outlook on life? Do you remember that feeling of freedom when the world was your oyster? Go back to that time and just hang out there with those feelings for awhile. As you remember those times and feel the emotions they invoke, know that they are happening right now, in your mind and remember....your mind doesn't know the difference between a memory and reality. This is proven. Your mind thinks that all those good things are happening right now. Know also that "like attracts like" and that the more you can be in those moments of well-being then the chances grow exponentially that you will be able to actualize those feelings into your reality. The same pattern will hold true for the angst, misery, and depression you relive. If you think about them too much, those too will come to pass.

So, there is no choice but to connect with others, and to rejoice as much as possible. If you can control your own mind to think and feel what you want it to, then you are in control and are not a victim of mind-control. The early days of being a victim of covert behavioral technologies are very confusing, heart-breaking, and painful and you'll probably do a lot of research during this time. However, you'll need to move on with your life if you want to overcome the victimization.

The sooner the better. Accept that people can be easily convinced and talked into doing all kinds of horrendous things, and that homo sapiens are a very imperfect species, you included. Accept it's happening. Then, wherever possible, move on to fix it even if that means adjusting your own focus and attitude and controlling what you want to think about.

I realize that is seems like a daunting task but there are tools to help you. Learn yoga, and practice envisioning something in your mind that's good and positive in nature for at least 5 minutes, non-stop, once a day. Within a few weeks to a few months you will be able to feel a difference. Then, start doing the meditation twice a day for five minutes each time. Keep advancng in the fashion until you hit 20 minutes twice a day. If your mind drifts away that's okay. Just gently bring it back but just make sure the meditation is for exactly 5 minutes. Time it. Set an alarm, and turn off your phone so as to have no interruptions. If you can do this daily you are on your way to controlling your own mind. Your enemies are always working towards pulling you into the hole with them. Don't go.

Do you remember what exhilarated and excited you before the harassment started? Go do that again sometime. Whether it's a game you like to play, or a walk around the neighborhood, or writing, or doing research and exploration, do it. It's a very good to force yourself to do things you're afraid to do, for one reason or another. Let go of the feeling of failure and dive into it, whatever it is. There are times when you're going to get frustrated with "their" efforts to discourage you but keep going, even if you're going a bit slower.

Find Love

Find love in any form you can. You will need it now. Of course, if you have or can find someone with good soul mate potential, that would be excellent and you should never give up hoping for it. Even if you never find a good mate for yourself it's best to keep dating or otherwise communicating with new people.

Having a pet for a friend has kept many a person from abject loneliness and I recommend it. However, if having a pet means that you'll have to be homeless because you can't find a roommate who'll take pets, I'd reconsider. You must be able to take care of yourself before anything else and it shows good judgement to do so. If having a pet ties you down too much, you may have to put it on the back burner, as well.

Never talk with others about being targeted except in passing. Like, you can say that you're experiencing some whistleblower retaliation but it's not a big deal. Say it's just "a little" slander and some people are trying to get in your way, and then drop it. If others probe you just tell them you don't feel like talking about it and it's no big deal anyway. Many a relationship has ended because targets confide too much in others about this problem. They're looking for a solution to the problem and for help, essentially, and to get the bad feelings out of their system. Almost always, friends and relatives start to fall off their social calendar, and sometimes the constant obsession with the harassment causes a divorce or domestic break. Don't risk it. There are others you can speak with about the problem without dumping all you rage and fear on people you care about.

Volunteering can also bring you closer to others and it has the added effect of alleviating depression and making you healthier, and you may meet some really good people while doing it. There are many places that accept volunteers like hospitals and retirement homes to soup kitchens and homeless shelters, and even Salvation Army Centers, and the like. Find your niche as a volunteer if you need some comradery.

Or simply go sit on your front porch and say hello to people passing by. If someone looks like they want to talk, great. Invite them over. Talk to anybody about anything except targeting, politics, and religion. Ask benign questions and offer water or some refreshment. Just talk, listen, and be gracious and that's all you have to do to get a friendship going.

Remember, you are not an island and you need interaction with other living things in order to remain healthy psychologically and physically. Animals are great but it's good to be able to socialize with other people. Some have devoted their lives to learning how to socialize. It's a great gift and it can be learned.. Regardless of how uncomfortable socializing makes you feel, keep working on those social skills. Do a search on Youtube for "learning social skills." Making others feel comfortable emotionally by smiling (being non-threatening), physically (offer refreshment), and being fun and/or sharing interesting thoughts and ideas is a good start. Having poor social skills in psychological terms is thought of as a, Social Learning Disorder, and it's often confused with other types of mental illnesses, such as schizophrenia.

The last word on the subject is that being unable to socialize is unhealthy in innumerable ways and causes a cascade of many problems. So, go out and start getting involved with others. If you don't know how then learn how to be effective socially to find happiness and community . Keep it light and easy and fun.

(https://www.psychologytoday.com/articles/200307/the-dangers-loneliness)

Look Amazing

Someone once told me that if I were to go out wearing super, top-of-the-line, expensive clothing, and had a great haircut and great make-up and accessories, that I could defecate in the middle of the street and get away with it. I laughed but the more I thought about this observation the more it seemed like a statement of fact rather than just a funny witticism. I realized that this is the reason why gangstalkers vandalize a targeted individual's belongings. They want you to appear unattractive in as many ways as possible and clothing has a lot to do with it. Obviously, making a target socially unappealing is high on the list of your enemies. This is exactly the reason why you have to make that special effort.

Many targets just want to give up. They've been brainwashed to give up through variety of methods. If the harassment completely ends because you let yourself go with regards to dress and appearance then do it. However, if the harassment continues no matter what you do then what's the point? It's a slippery slope and if you give in on one thing you'll give in on others. Drag yourself to any clothing or big box store and check out the sale racks. The prices often rival those in the 2nd hand stores. Also, don't underestimate places like K-Mart or Wal-Mart. Once in awhile it's just what the doctor ordered. Know what to spend money on and what you can pull off cheaply because you know it's just a matter of time before you might be vandalized again.

Don't forget about making the most out of make-up, hair styles, and of being well groomed, for both men and women. Being in style and age appropriate is a plus. Get some tips off the internet about hair styles. Learn how to cut your own hair, or put it up if you're a woman. Enjoy being creative about what you look like and how you're coming off. Try different things but keep your style appropriate for street wear, date wear, and business wear and utilize all three.

Don't Get Paranoid

A lot of the covert harassment and surveillance is organized around making the target appear to have either paranoid schizophrenia, or any one of the paranoid or delusional disorders. The harassment, surveillance, and attacks are centered around this. The reason your enemies want to make you look paranoid is to discredit your perceptions and your word. In essence, and for all intents and purposes, it's used to silence people, and to make them ineffectual. Now, on the bright side, if you want to call it that, I've heard that once some targets get diagnosed with a psychological disorder the harassment lightens up, particularly if they also stop socializing and give up on their dreams. I make no judgement calls about people who need a break from the harassment and go this route. If you're happy and you've learned to function well in all areas but within certain limits then good. You've made the right decision. However, others would have a hard time surviving with a psychological diagnosis.

If you feel like you need to be effectual and credible then pay attention to your verbalizations and reactions. Don't act paranoid, like don't turn down invitations because you want to stay in the house to make sure no one comes in, or touches anything. Don't stop using cell phones and computers because you think they've been compromised because without the benefit of modern conveniences you're not going to be successful in any way.

Here's a list of things targeted individuals are often frightened into doing that make them look paranoid or unreasonable.

1. They stay at home all of the time.
2. They obsessively try to convince everyone that they're being stalked, harassed and under surveillance around the clock. They refuse to drop the issue.
3. They give up on their hopes, dreams, and goals.
4. They pay less attention to their cleanliness, and general upkeep.
5. They stop using, or are continuously buying new computers and cell phones because of digital hacking and harassment.
6. They stop looking for meaningful work, or figuring out ways to make money.
7. Targets often get obsessed with what the harassment program is about and how to stop it to the exclusion of responsibilities and social expectations.
8. They may act paranoid by speaking furtively and in hushed voices or only under certain circumstances, out of fear of being listened in on.
9. They don't trust anyone and look for reasons not to.
10. They string coincidences or incidents together to create a story or scenario that coincides with their beliefs, with scant or no evidence.
11. Targets might continuously call, write, and text complaints to many people whom they believe can help stop the abuse. While the abuse may slow down for awhile telling others may also speed it up. I've never heard that phone calls and letters have stopped the abuse.

Under the circumstances of being targeted, I would consider all of these aforementioned behaviors to be normal. The environment of the target is abnormal and the target reacts accordingly. However, the targeting program does drive people to display verbal and physical behaviors that can give a false positive if tested for paranoia. These behaviors have to be overcome if the target wants to be successful or have meaningful relationships because they are confining and limit a person's movement and outreach to others.

Keep Fighting for Your Freedom-Never Give Up

This is far too horrendous a crime to pretend it doesn't exist but the integrity of this battle depends on your presentation of the facts, and to whom you're presenting them. I have a client who made flyers about simple gang-stalking and mobbing and sent them out to numerous people in positions of authority including the Police Chief, and the Mayor of his hometown. Within a few days a cop and another guy from the city showed up at his front door and wanted to give him a mental evaluation right then. He refused and so they took him to a jail cell that had no running water or sanitary toilets and the next morning had a Medical Doctor (not even a psychologist) diagnose him with a paranoid disorder after talking to him for only 5 minutes.

This is a cautionary, true tale to warn you about what can happen if you go public about the harassment and abuse you're suffering under. Unfortunately, it seems like any complaint you make about the harassment can be perceived as paranoid according to the limited perceptions, experience and knowledge of most people who are educated in psychology. On occasion, you'll find a knowledgeable and honest professional who'll acknowledge that mobbing, stalking, and harassment can happen if you get on someone's bad side but only if you present it logically and without any hysteria or mania. In order to do this it helps if you know why you're being attacked. It also helps to get some coaching from someone like myself before you confide in others.

If you became a targeted individual because you complained about any person, corporation, or business to law-enforcement, or to any other authority figure, government agency, watchdog agency, or human relations office you can tell others that you suffering to do whistleblower retaliation because of a complaint you've made. This explanation will legitimize the harassment you're experiencing in a way that others can understand.

Whatever the reason for your targeting you can legitimize it. There are always several reasons why someone might be targeted and those can be figured into the explanation of why you're being targeted. It's very highly recommended that targets get a professional consultation before spilling their guts so they don't come off as paranoid.

Unfortunately, and no matter how true, using the explanation that you're a government experiment may work if you're on a talk show about conspiracy theories but it might not get you too far under most circumstances because it's an unusual claim and as such requires evidence. While experimentation by governments, corporations, or individuals may be the reason for the targeting, if you walk into a police station and say tell them that their going to ask you if you're on medication for a psychiatric disorder. Being able to see what kind of an effect your words have on others is really important here. Knowing what to say, what not to say, how to say it, and to whom is so important. The program is constructed to make the target look paranoid so try to stick with things that sound familiar. I've rarely heard of a case where law enforcement was able to help to stop the stalking and abuse, anyway. While there are cops who want to help they are often at a loss.

All About You

How you present yourself to the world at large can make a big difference in how things end up for you. Presenting yourself to others as kind and generous is the ideal but sometimes the warrior in you may slip out, which can be a good thing if you're intimidating enough to scare the perps away without getting arrested. It can be a good thing to appear threatening if it means that your stalkers will back off but I've never known this to happen. You stalkers have already been told that you're evil, dangerous, and have to be contained, punished, and disposed of into an institution of some sort. Acting like you're bad could give your stalkers more fodder for a kill effect. You're proving what is being said about you.

I think that it really frustrates and angers the stalkers is if you don't care and you continue to go on with your life as planned. To act like you don't even know you're being stalked and harassed but instead act like you think that you have a medical problem and a string of bad luck. This must be incredibly frustrating for your enemies and they'll probably entertain you by acting out to the max. I mean, they want you to think someone's out to get you so they might double up their efforts. You know what they say about giving them enough rope to hang themselves? Well, they sometimes do. They'll take greater and greater chances more often just to get you to notice them. Sometimes playing dumb is the way to go if you want to catch them However, most targets realize this too late.

There is another way is to behave that can draw them out and that's to act like you just don't care and that you have zilch interest in their stupidity and criminal behavior, and that they can have at it because you're busy having a life. Make sure you have people around you and that you stay busy. Again, they will continue to act out but will take more chances and will be more obvious. There's something in the psyche of gangstalkers that makes them want to be noticed. They can be like 3-year-olds who want attention, "Look at me, look at me." This character flaw can be the key to getting some evidence on the gangstalkers. It's also very entertaining because they will run around in circles for you. It's can be like watching a movie featuring The Three Stooges, or The Keystone Cops. However, don't let your guard down because these are also the traits of guys with dangerous personality disorders.

Gangstalkers and the perpetrators of covert harassment and surveillance are terrorists to the nines and that's their job. They exist to terrorize people. They are truly the representatives of the definition of domestic terrorism. However, they are not assassins, per se. Many targets think that the stalkers want to assassinate them but they will not. Even if they want to it's not part of the program. They want to terrorize and sicken you, perhaps. They want to drive you to the physician's office, the psychiatrist's office, and to the dental office but that's for monetary gain more then anything in the bigger picture. That's the reason for everything that they do. If you can blow them off psychologically, and use self care, you'd be on the right track. I spoke to a client recently who told me that he just gave up and thought that if they want to come after him they can have at it. He went to bed with all his doors unlocked and open and felt that if they killed him it would be a blessing. Well, they didn't. He's alive but the terrorism has gotten to him a little. He's unable to work because of the harassment. They didn't kill him though and they never will. It's not part of the program.

Remember that even with all the scare tactics, confusing antics, vandalism, street theater, etc., they won't kill you outright. They can cause damage through exposure to biological and chemical infectants, and through remote weapons but I'm not quite sure if they're wearing down the targets or building up their immune systems. Take your vitamins and anti-inflammatories every day and in the end we'll see what the effects are. I already spoke of the physical and psychological effects of doing good, and doing evil and these are variables that the perpetrators of this brand of domestic terrorism haven't taken into account. We'll have to wait until it all pans out but personally, I know targets who are living very long lives.

Aim For Success and Don't Give Up

Apparently, one of the larger reasons why gangstalking program exists, and what they are trying to do is to induce you to give up on everything, which is a by-product of depression. It's worth repeating…. don't ever go there. Every day do something to promote yourself. Always continue to strive for financial gain in any way that you can, even if you're selling pencils you got from the dollar store. Promote yourself or your product on blogs and social media, etc. Don't give up looking for love and stay in the game, keep at your dreams of success, and don't forget to enjoy the simple things like a beautiful morning, or a full moon on a clear night. Enjoy and be grateful for what you have regardless of how little it is. If you have a roof over your head and food to eat then you are already successful. Just build on that. Go look in the mirror and repeat loudly in a strong voice, "I am a good person and I am worthy of everything that I want" and then keep saying it. Say it until you feel it. Say daily until you're sick of saying it, then do it again the next day. This can work miracles.

Also, let's not forget that there's a karmic, spiritual component to all of this. I've never seen a case of gangstalking where the sins of the target exceeded the sins of the stalker. Regardless of what the so-called reason for the terrorist activity against the victim is, it never quite measures up to the wrong-doing that the terrorists are doing.

Targeting Women

Women talk and everyone knows it. It's genetic. Girls learn to talk earlier than boys do on average. I'm sure the reasons for this attribute figure into child-rearing and maybe even into leadership abilities, and we have to accept it as a fact of nature. We also have to accept that women have an ingrained component to nurture others. They make chicken soup, give you vitamins, see if you have a fever, tell you that everything's going to be okay, etc. It's what they do. These two seemingly benevolent attributes, when combined, can be thought of as dangerous, and are often the reasons why women so easily become the victims of domestic terrorism. They want to save people and animals close to themselves, and they often want to save wildlife and the Earth, in general. It's true that women can be diverted from their natural selves and turn into autotrons but nature usually wins that battle in the end, or at least we hope it does. By the way, many men also have these attributes and they get into just as much trouble and their female counterparts.

So, because of this compassion and desire to assist others, and to right what's wrong, women often become whistleblowers. It's true that women blow the whistle more often than men and it's at this point that the life preserving feminine attributes of nurturing and communication are perverted and redefined as "troublemaking." Well, if working to ensure clean air, water, land, and food for me and my family, and if addressing greed that's propagated at the cost of misery and suffering, and if reporting dangerous criminal activity is being a troublemaker, then please be a troublemaker.

We're at a point in our growth and evolution as a species where some hard decisions have to be made. We've known for decades that the path we've decided to take with fossil fuels and corporate farming was going down a dirty path but we didn't think it was going to lead us to the forest of no return. We always thought we could rebalance the environment but now we're not so sure. Many think it's already too late but it's natural to try to rectify things. As far as the corporations telling us that we can handle breathing a little dirty air or drinking a little dirty water, or that it's okay to let entire classes of life go extent, or that it's okay for the oceans to die for reasons of financial gain, I'd have to disagree. Add me to the list of troublemakers.

Further, It's slowly becoming a fairly well-known fact by people who are employed in facilities that work to protect women from domestic violence, and deranged ex-boyfriends that gangstalking and harassment is a real phenomenon. The covert criminal stalking, and criminal harassment and abuse of women with biological.chemical compounds, and remote weapons is a great way for psychologically twisted men to continue to commit violence against the object of their fantasies and obsessions, and to continue to maim, torture, and destroy them and not get apprehended and punished for doing so. The fact of the matter is that if a man is capable of brutalizing an ex wife or girlfriend like this then that explains the reason why she left him to begin with. A man doesn't change from a compassionate and loving man into a heinous gang-stalking monster overnight. The question is what is the fear that lies behind the stalking?

Back in the 1960's and 70's, during the days of cointelpro, the women's political movement was under heavy attack by the government who felt that to give women equal rights and equal pay would somehow mess up the economy and society, in general. It makes me now wonder if there's some version of cointelpro going on wherein government factions want to force women to stay with violent and abusive men for some nebulous and obscure reason, that we don't know about. Is it just that bad guys find and work with other bad guys? Is it something more and when do we start protecting women from men who appear to be going on destructive, and often murderous wildings against them?

Over-all, women are the victims of covert harassment and surveillance about twice as much as men are. We know by the stats that it's not because they are considered terrorists in the traditional sense of the word. They aren't out there toting machine guns or ramming vans with explosives into government buildings. That's strictly a guy thing. Sometimes, terrorists can force a female at gun-point to strap herself with explosives and wander out into a crowd but as evidenced by reports and video, it appears that women are forced to do this. As for American born women doing such nonsense...no, it's not going to happen. Rather, women can be considered terrorists because they might expose child abuse in the church or within some other power structure, elder abuse, client abuse, poisoned water and air, etc. This is how American women, and women in general world-wide, get on someone's dirt list.

Whistle-blowing by women seems to be proliferating and it's becoming apparent that intimidation isn't working, over-all. I'm not sure why but I think that outrage and action against the abuse of others, or against the destruction of the environment is ingrained or genetic. As the environment continues to disentegrate, more and more people are going to stand up against those who are destroying it and I don't think there's much anyone can do to stop them. Many men are a huge part of this movement and have accessed the side of themselves that represents nurturning and compassion.

The Cost of Control

The cost of controlling the population has many variables. Among them are government agencies who get federal funding to police the population via citizen patrol and citizen policing groups, contractors who get work from private and public sectors to go after whistleblowers and complainers, criminal elements who use the technology to control their victims, and attorneys whose job includes discrediting witnesses, are the more common venues for stopping the walk of "undesirables" and "trouble-makers". The cost does run into the millions of dollars at this level. Cheap help is easy to come by and it's easy for contractors to make a good living providing they use needy, poor, addicted, homeless, and lonely people as their street soldiers. That way they don't have to pay a lot to get the job done. Ten or twenty dollars or less per day is about all it takes for those who demand payment, and many people will work for free if they're lonely and need to belong to a group, or if they're angry, or bored.

What we hear from those who have been sought out to do gang-stalking, and highway mobbing has been laughable. One guy in New York who's going to college to become an attorney had been offered $20.00 a day to drive around and harass people. Shortly after he refused he began to get gangstalked, himself. There are other similar stories about the street level pay of gang-stalkers. They may get a car to drive around in while they're "working" but it's often from a dealership, or rental, or just a piece of unregistered junk.

Some street stalkers are offered porn, or drugs, or friendship as an incentive to join the club, and a cheap hire. Then if the target moves out of range all the perks are withdrawn because it's about the bottom line, and the bottom line has to do with money and cheap or free help.

Apparently, it doesn't take much to get people to commit atrocities against their neighbors, as evidenced by the Milgram Experiment https://www.sciencedaily.com/releases/2017/03/170314081558.htm   However, the good news is that, according to the experimental results, about 33 per cent of any population cannot be talked into hurting someone else, even if an authority figure tells them to. That's a lot of people. Further, offshoots of the original experiment have shown that if one person openly refuses to participate in the destruction of another person on moral or religious grounds, everyone who witnesses the refusal will also refuse to participate in the abuses. One person can make a difference.

Psychological Effects of Gangstalking and of Covert Harassment and Surveillance

Going through psychological and physical harassment 24/7 for days, weeks, and years can take it's toll. Some people do well and others, not so well. The harassment is meant to draw the target into a state of paranoia and delusional thinking. It's done by causing confusion, fear, depersonalization, and derealization. If targets get too caught up in the harassment, and if they perceive their lives to balance on the opinions of other people, they can get into a loop of wondering how, why, what, who, when, and where, that is never-ending and extremely damaging. In order to avoid this trap it's important to seek out people who are experts or are well-known in the field so that victims can go on with their lives as best as they can. Don't stop your life. It's good to get some info on the subject and to keep in touch with experts who can help you to understand what's happening to you, but don't trade in your dreams for the twisted nightmares of the bad guys.

People can invite paranoia into their lives by simply thinking too much about anything they consider strange. For example, if you come home one day and find that your bathtub is scratched and busted in places it wasn't when you left that morning, your reaction should be, "Hmmm. Weird," and that's it. Unless you have it on video, or unless a neighbor tells you that someone was in your home, all the paranoid thoughts you might have are a waste of time. Calling the cops may be a waste of time because you don't have the evidence. If you're concerned talk to a security specialist or buy some locks (this usually doesn't help). Do what you have to do and then move on. Your stalkers want you to spend all of your precious time, to the point of obsession, just thinking about them and their strange antics. Don't do it. **Their punishment is that they're throwing their lives away obsessing about you.** Official recognition of the the crime and of the criminals is what we all seek but in the meantime, keep walking.

Also, many targets are prone to panic attacks. These are commonly mistaken for heart attacks and targets will often seek out medical help for an ailing heart after experiencing a panic attack only to be told by the attending physicians that there's nothing wrong with their heart. (https://www.adaa.org/living-with-anxiety/ask-and-learn/ask-expert/how-can-i-tell-if-%E2%80%99m-having-panic-attack-or-heart-atta) At this time it would be wise to go to a general practitioner of medicine and tell him or her about the symptoms, but refrain from giving your imput about what you think the problem is. Also, it's not a good idea to talk about the gangstalking. Or, if you prefer you can get something over-the counter like valerian root and see what happens. If the feeling of cardiac distress diminishes after taking anti-anxiety herbs or drugs then celebrate. You've ruled out a major concern. Believe me, when I say that 24/7 surveillance, harassment, vandalism, hacking, slander, and sleep deprivation can take it's toll and anyone can easily devolve into an anxious state. Just know that it's temporary and that it's something that can be overcome through diet, exercise, consultations, and a mild sedative.

Being gang-stalked is like being in a war because just like soldiers, targets never know when or where the next attack will happen and so they are always on guard, especially in the beginning of the targeting. This kind of vigilance can lead to exhaustion and sometimes to Post-Traumatic-Stress-Disorder. Targets can eventually resume normalcy if they refuse to waste time thinking about the behaviors of others, especially if those behaviors are merely attitudes and opinions. Any type of invasion of the body or mind without consent, including biological/chemical attacks, and remote weapons' attacks, should be checked out and efforts made to put an end to it. However, don't let the war take you down with your enemies. It sometimes seems that all they do is think about you, however you should be thinking about improving your life in any way possible.

The Last Word

In the end, the thing that's going to save you is Love; love from friends, love from family, love from pets, and love from those who work with the targets of gangstalking. Sometimes I think, however, that it's more about the love that we give to others that saves us. When we love on others, whether it's on people, pets, or the Earth in general, we are nourished in ways that affect us positively physically and psychologically.

Stay on good terms with others as much as possible, smile as much as you can muster, and go forward with your life. Let no one stop you or turn you aside. You will walk slower, maybe, or maybe this ordeal will lead you into new directions where you may prosper in several ways. Whatever you do, don't lay down and roll over. We'll all be gone soon enough and there's no sense in practicing for it now.

If they're watching, let them if you can't do otherwise but never stop; never say die. Fight to the end. I'm with you in spirit.

Special thanks to the following people for educating me with their brilliant videos, presentations, and conferences, and for working with me in my efforts to help the victims and their families.

Eleanor White

Derrick Robinson

James Walbert

John Hall

Jesse Beltran

Robert Duncan

Made in the USA
Coppell, TX
24 February 2021

tabulated below, and their names are transliterated by using the *pinyin* due to the absence of English equivalents:

Relating to the positions

Symbol	Name and Meaning
0	The position at the ledges
I	The 1st position at the frets
II	The 2nd position at the frets
III	The 3rd position at the frets
IV	The 4th position at the frets

Relating to the strings

Symbol	Name and Meaning
—	*Zi xian*/子弦, the 1st string
‖	*Zhong xian*/中弦, the 2nd string
≣	*Lao xian*/老弦, the 3rd string
X	*Chan xian*/纏弦, the 4th string
( )	Open string; used with the above four signs to indicate which string is not to be pressed

Relating to the left hand

Symbol	Name	Meaning
一	1st finger	Press the string with the index finger
二	2nd finger	Press the string with the middle finger
三	3rd finger	Press the string with the ring finger
四	4th finger	Press the string with the little finger
	Yin/吟, *rou*/揉	Apply vibrato by shaking the hand to produce a wave-like note. Shaking horizontally is called *yin*, while shaking vertically is called *rou*
↔	*Bai*/擺	Apply vibrato with larger amplitude by shaking the hand horizontally
	Dai/帶	Pluck the string to produce a sound after playing a note thereon
	Sou/摄	Scratch the string with a finger to produce sounds
	Da/打	Hit a fret with pressure to produce sounds
	Tui/推, *la*/拉	Raise the pitch of the note by temporarily distorting the string. Pushing the string inward is called *tui*, while pulling the string outward is called *la*
→	*Chou*/綽, *zhu*/注	Apply glissandos with a finger sliding on the string. Sliding from a lower note to a higher note is called *chou*, while its opposite is called *zhu*
	Ya/壓	Press the string vigorously to raise the pitch of the note

	Zhuang/撞	Apply *tui* or *la* and then return to the previous pitch
⤴	Zhuang/撞	Apply *tui* or *la* and then return to the previous pitch
⽊	Le/勒	Clamp the strings with two fingers (either the index and middle fingers, or the middle and ring fingers)
tr	Trill	Press the string at adjacent ledges/ frets in multiple alternations rapidly
O	Harmonics	Press the string at a natural harmonic point

Miscellaneous

Symbol	Name	Meaning
⼤	*Jiaoerxian/* 絞二弦	Twist the 1ˢᵗ and 2ⁿᵈ strings together, with either string on top of another
⼤	*Jiaosanxian/* 絞三弦	Twist the 1ˢᵗ, 2ⁿᵈ and 3ʳᵈ strings together, with the 1ˢᵗ string under the other two strings or vice versa
⼤	*Jiaosixian* 絞四弦	Twist all the four strings together

<u>Relating to the right hand</u>

Of the index finger

Symbol	Name	Meaning
＼	*Tan/*彈	Pluck the string outward in the direction of right to left from the player's point of view
＼＼	*Shuangtan/* 雙彈	Similar to *tan*, but pluck two neighboring strings simultaneously to produce a sound

Symbol	Name	Meaning
ꟿ	Xiaosao/小掃	Similar to *tan*, but pluck three strings simultaneously to produce a sound
ꟿ	Sao/掃	Similar to *tan*, but pluck all the four strings simultaneously to produce a sound
)	Mo/抹	Pluck the string inward in the direction of left to right from the player's point of view
↑	Gua/掛	Pluck the strings from the inner to outer ones to achieve the arpeggio effect

Of the thumb

Symbol	Name	Meaning
/	Tiao/挑	Pick the string outward in the direction of left to right from the player's point of view
//	Shuangtiao/雙挑	Similar to *tiao*, but pick two neighboring strings simultaneously to produce a sound
ꟿ	Xiaofu/小拂	Similar to *tiao*, but pick three strings simultaneously to produce a sound
ꟿ	Fu/拂	Similar to *tiao*, but pick all the four strings simultaneously to produce a sound
(	Gou/勾	Pick the string inward in the direction of right to left from the player's point of view
↓	Lin/臨	Pick the strings from the outer to inner ones to achieve the arpeggio effect

Of the middle finger

Symbol	Name	Meaning
ꞱＬ	Ti/剔	Pluck the string outward in the direction of right to left from the player's point of view

⟍	*Zhongzhimo/* 中指抹	Pick the string inward in the direction of left to right from the player's point of view

Of tremolo variations

Symbol	Name	Meaning
⊢⊂ or ⫽	*Yaozhi/* 搖指	Pluck the string rapidly and continuously with any of the four fingers, with the nail at an angle to the string, such that the string seems to shake sideway
⋇	*Lun/*輪	Pluck the string outward with all of the four fingers from right to left in order, and end with the thumb picking from left to right from the player's point of view, whereby producing a tremolo effect
⋇⋯	*Changlun/* 長輪	Repeat *lun* for several times
⁃⦁⁃	*Banlun/* 半輪	Similar to *lun*, except that the thumb is not involved in the cycle
⁃⦁⁃⋯	*Sizhi changlun/* 四指長輪	Repeat *banlun* for several times
⋏	*Sanzhi lun/* 三指輪	Pluck the string outward with the index and middle fingers from right to left in order, and end with the thumb picking from left to right from the player's point of view, whereby producing a tremolo effect
⋏⋯	*Sanzhi changlun/* 三指長輪	Repeat *sanzhi lun* for several times

Miscellaneous

Symbol	Name	Meaning
L	*Pai/*拍	Pick the string upward with the thumb and release it immediately
⊦	*Tanmianban/* 彈面板	Hit the front panel with the nail of the thumb or index finger
⊥	*Lunban/* 輪板	Similar to *lun*, but act on the front panel instead of the strings
◇○◇	Artificial harmonics	With a finger of the left hand substituting the nut, press the string at 1/2 or 1/3 with the right little finger and pluck the string with the right index finger to produce an artificial harmonic

The list is not exhaustive owing to the plethora of pipa-specific marks. The descriptions of most right-handed skills listed in the above table should speak for themselves, while some of them like the tremolo variations and the majority of left-handed skills require more practices, so will not be discussed further in view of their technical difficulty.   In the meantime, if you are able to read the above sheet music without any trouble, we can move on to the next stage to begin practicing with the fingering chart.

The Key Signatures of the Pipa

Theoretically speaking, we can play all the 12 majors (A, B, C, D, E, F, G and A♭, B♭, D♭, E♭, G♭) with the pipa, but usually we only play five of them (D, G, F, C and A) that are present in the traditional *Gongche* notation (工尺譜), which comprises seven keys:

Name	Notation	Corresponding Key in Modern Western Music
Xiao Gong Diao/小工調	1 = D	D
Zheng Gong Diao/正宮調	1 = G	G
Liu Zi Diao/六字調	1 = F	F
Chi Zi Diao/尺字調	1 = C	C
Fan Zi Diao/凡字調	1 = E♭	E♭
Yi Zi Diao/乙字調	1 = A	A
Shang Zi Diao/上字調	1 = B♭	B♭

Among the seven keys of this notation, *Fan Zi Diao* and *Shang Zi Diao* are rare for the pipa.   Therefore, we are left with the aforesaid five key signatures.

The four strings of the pipa are by default tuned at A2, D3, E3 and A3 under most circumstances.   Nevertheless, other settings such as (G, D, E, A), (B, D, E, A), (A, #C, E, A) are also available for particular songs. At the beginner stage, we do not have to change the default setting, under which the D major is the fundamental key.

Consequently, we shall look into these 5 majors each by each, with the D major being the first one.

The D Major

The fingering for the D major is shown below:

	4th string	3rd string	2nd string	1st string		Position
Nut	5	1	2	5	Open String	
1st ledge						
2nd ledge	6	2	3	6	一	
3rd ledge			4		二	0
4th ledge	7	3		7		
5th ledge	1	4	5	1	三	
6th ledge						
1st fret	2	5	6	2	四/一	
2nd fret						
3rd fret	3	6	7	3	二	I
4th fret	4		1	4	三	
5th fret		7				
6th fret	5	1	2	5	四/一	
7th fret						
8th fret	6	2	3	6	二	II
9th fret			4		三	
10th fret	7	3		7		
11th fret	1	4	5	1	四/一	
12th fret						
13th fret	2	5	6	2	二	
14th fret						III
15th fret	3	6	7	3	三	
16th fret	4		1	4	四	
17th fret		7				
18th fret	5	1	2	5	一	
19th fret						
20th fret		2	3	6	二	IV
21st fret			4		三	
22nd fret		3		7		
23rd fret		4	5	1	四	
24th fret						

Unlike bow-stringed instruments (i.e. the erhu/ violin's family), the notes of the pipa can be played easily by pressing the corresponding ledges/ frets, which are clearly separated from each other by a semitone.

The notes of the 1st and 4th strings share the same fingering but differ by an octave, whereas the notes of the 2nd and 3rd strings differ by a tone.

33

In the following, I will show the fingering of the ledges and the 1st position of the frets, as the other positions of the frets just repeat the same pattern downward.

The 0th position

The open strings (without pressing any ledges/ frets) will produce the A2, D3, E3 and A3 notes, and the corresponding solfeggi are "5", "1", "2" and "5".

Pressing the four strings at the 2nd ledge with the 1st finger will produce the B2, E3, F$^{#}$3 and B3 notes, and the corresponding solfeggi are "6", "2", "3" and "6" (The right picture shows the 1st finger pressing the 1st string).

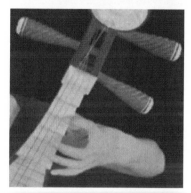

Pressing the 2nd string at the 3rd ledge and the 4th, 3rd and 1st strings at the 4th ledge with the 2nd finger will produce the G3, C$^{#}$3, F$^{#}$3 and C$^{#}$4 notes respectively, while the corresponding solfeggi are "4", "7", "3" and "7" (The right picture shows the 2nd finger pressing the 2nd string).

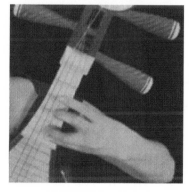

Pressing the four strings at the 5th ledge with the 3rd finger will produce the D3, G3, A3 and D4 notes, and the corresponding solfeggi are "1", "4", "5" and "1" (The right picture shows the 3rd finger pressing the 4th string).

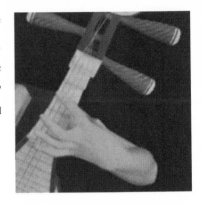

The 1st position

Pressing the four strings at the 1st fret with the 1st finger will produce the E3, A3, B3 and E4 notes, and the corresponding solfeggi are "2", "5", "6" and "2" (The left picture shows the 1st finger pressing the 1st string).

Pressing the four strings at the 3rd fret with the 2nd finger will produce the $F^{\#}3$, B3, $C^{\#}4$ and $F^{\#}4$ notes, and the corresponding solfeggi are "3", "6", "7" and "3" (The left picture shows the 2nd finger pressing the 1st string).

Pressing the 4th, 2nd and 1st strings at the 4th fret and the 3rd string at the 5th fret with the 3rd finger will produce the G3, D4, G4 and C#4 notes respectively, while the corresponding solfeggi are "4", "1" "4" and "7" (The left picture shows the 3rd finger pressing the 1st string).

Pressing the four strings at the 6th fret with the 4th finger will produce the A3, D4, E4 and A4 notes, and the corresponding solfeggi are "5", "1", "2" and "5" (The left picture shows the 4th finger pressing the 1st string). At this fret, we have raised the pitches of the notes on the four strings by an octave.

The following salient points apply to all majors:

1) The solfeggi "3", "4" and "7", "1" are a pair of semitones and are located on two adjacent ledges/ frets;

2) The range of a pipa is from A2 (nut of the 4th string) to D#6 (24th fret of the 1st string), in which there are 5 positions;

3) The II, III, IV and V position always start at 1st, 6th, 11th and 18th frets irrespective of the majors; and

4) Very often, a note that can be played by pressing the ledges/ frets with the 4th finger can be played by using the 1st finger as well, save that we will change to the next position then.

36

The G Major

The fingering for the G major is shown below:

	4th string	3rd string	2nd string	1st string		Position
Nut	2	5	6	2	Open String	
1st ledge						
2nd ledge	3	6	7	3	一	
3rd ledge	4		1	4	二	0
4th ledge		7				
5th ledge	5	1	2	5	三	
6th ledge						
1st fret	6	2	3	6	四/一	
2nd fret			4		二	
3rd fret	7	3		7		I
4th fret	1	4	5	1	三	
5th fret						
6th fret	2	5	6	2	四/一	
7th fret						
8th fret	3	6	7	3	二	
9th fret	4		1	4	三	II
10th fret		7				
11th fret	5	1	2	5	四/一	
12th fret						
13th fret	6	2	3	6	二	
14th fret			4		三	III
15th fret	7	3		7		
16th fret	1	4	5	1	四	
17th fret						
18th fret	2	5	6	2	一	
19th fret						
20th fret		6	7	3	二	IV
21st fret			1	4	三	
22nd fret		7				
23rd fret		1	2	5	四	
24th fret						

Similar to the D major, the open strings (without pressing any ledges/frets) will also produce A2, D3, E3 and A3 notes, but the corresponding solfeggi they represent are "2", "5", "6" and "2" this time.

The F Major

The fingering for the F major is shown below:

	4th string	3rd string	2nd string	1st string		Position
Nut	3	6	7	3	Open String	
1st ledge	4		1	4		
2nd ledge		7			一	
3rd ledge	5	1	2	5	二	0
4th ledge						
5th ledge	6	2	3	6	三	
6th ledge			4			
1st fret	7	3		7	四／一	
2nd fret	1	4	5	1	二	
3rd fret						
4th fret	2	5	6	2	三	I
5th fret						
6th fret	3	6	7	3	四／一	
7th fret	4		1	4	一	
8th fret		7				
9th fret	5	1	2	5	三	II
10th fret						
11th fret	6	2	3	6	四／一	
12th fret			4			
13th fret	7	3		7	一	
14th fret	1	4	5	1	三	III
15th fret						
16th fret	2	5	6	2	四	
17th fret						
18th fret	3	6	7	3	一	
19th fret			1	4		
20th fret		7			一	
21st fret		1	2	5	三	IV
22nd fret						
23rd fret		2	3	6	四	
24th fret						

For the F major, the corresponding solfeggi of the open strings are "3", "6", "7" and "3" this time. As the solfeggi "7" and "3" are semitones, we need to press the 1st ledge for the 1st and 2nd strings to produce another pair of semitones, the solfeggi "1" and "4" respectively.

The C Major

The fingering for the C major is shown below:

	4th string	3rd string	2nd string	1st string		Position
Nut	6	2	3	6	Open String	
1st ledge			4		一	
2nd ledge	7	3		7		
3rd ledge	1	4	5	1	二	0
4th ledge						
5th ledge	2	5	6	2	三	
6th ledge						
1st fret	3	6	7	3	四／一	
2nd fret	4		1	4	一	
3rd fret		7				I
4th fret	5	1	2	5	三	
5th fret						
6th fret	6	2	3	6	四／一	
7th fret			4		一	
8th fret	7	3		7		II
9th fret	1	4	5	1	三	
10th fret						
11th fret	2	5	6	2	四／一	
12th fret						
13th fret	3	6	7	3	二	III
14th fret	4		1	4	三	
15th fret		7				
16th fret	5	1	2	5	四	
17th fret						
18th fret	6	2	3	6	一	
19th fret			4		二	
20th fret		3		7		
21st fret		4	5	1	三	IV
22nd fret						
23rd fret		5	6	2	四	
24th fret						

For the C major, the corresponding solfeggi of the open strings are "6", "2", "3" and "6" this time. As the solfeggio "3" is a semitone, we need to press the 1st ledge for the 2nd string to produce another semitone, the solfeggio "4".

The A Major

The fingering for the A major is shown below:

	4th string	3rd string	2nd string	1st string		Position
Nut	1	4	5	1	Open String	
1st ledge						
2nd ledge	2	5	6	2	—	
3rd ledge						0
4th ledge	3	6	7	3	二	
5th ledge	4		1	4		
6th ledge		7			三	
1st fret	5	1	2	5	四/一	
2nd fret						
3rd fret	6	2	3	6	二	I
4th fret			4			
5th fret	7	3		7	三	
6th fret	1	4	5	1	四/一	
7th fret						
8th fret	2	5	6	2	—	II
9th fret						
10th fret	3	6	7	3	二	
11th fret	4		1	4	四/一	
12th fret		7			二	
13th fret	5	1	2	5		
14th fret						
15th fret	6	2	3	6	二	III
16th fret			4			
17th fret	7	3		7	四	
18th fret	1	4	5	1	—	
19th fret						
20th fret		5	6	2	二	
21st fret						IV
22nd fret		6	7	3	二	
23rd fret				1	4	四
24th fret						

For the A major, the corresponding solfeggi of the open strings are "1", "4", "5" and "1" this time. The arrangement of its fingering is akin to those of the D and G majors, in which the 1st ledge is not involved. We have hereby concluded all the five majors, and let's play some songs for practices now!

Selected Songs

旱天雷

Thunder in the Dry Season

Cantonese Folk Song

Stepping High

1=D (5̣ 1 2 5)

Cantonese Folk Song

Dance of the Golden Snake

Composed by Nie Er

1=D (5 1 2 5)

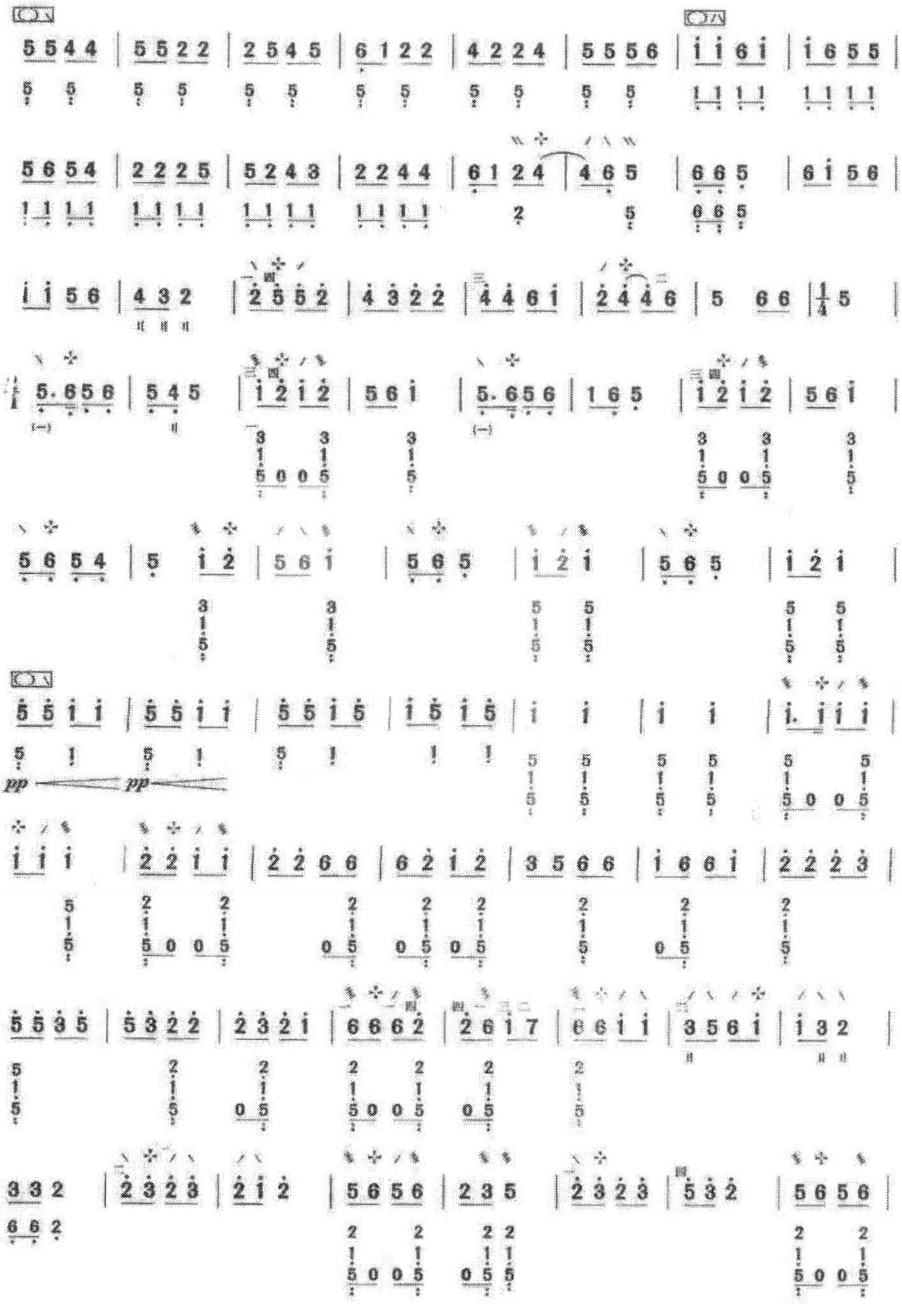

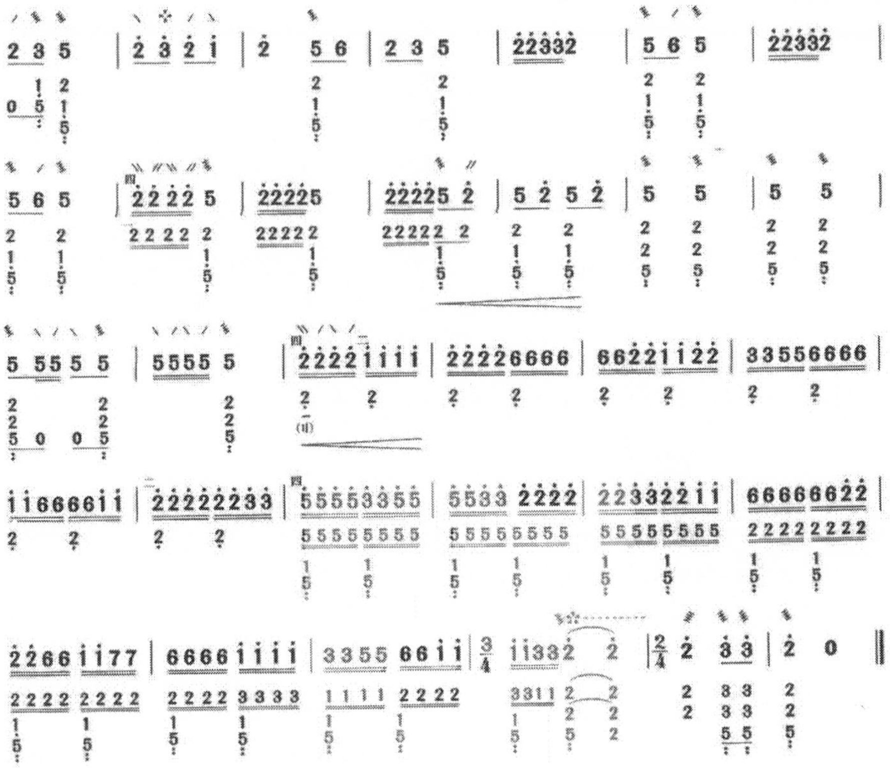

Deep Night

Beijing Opera Song

1=D 2/4 ♩ = 96

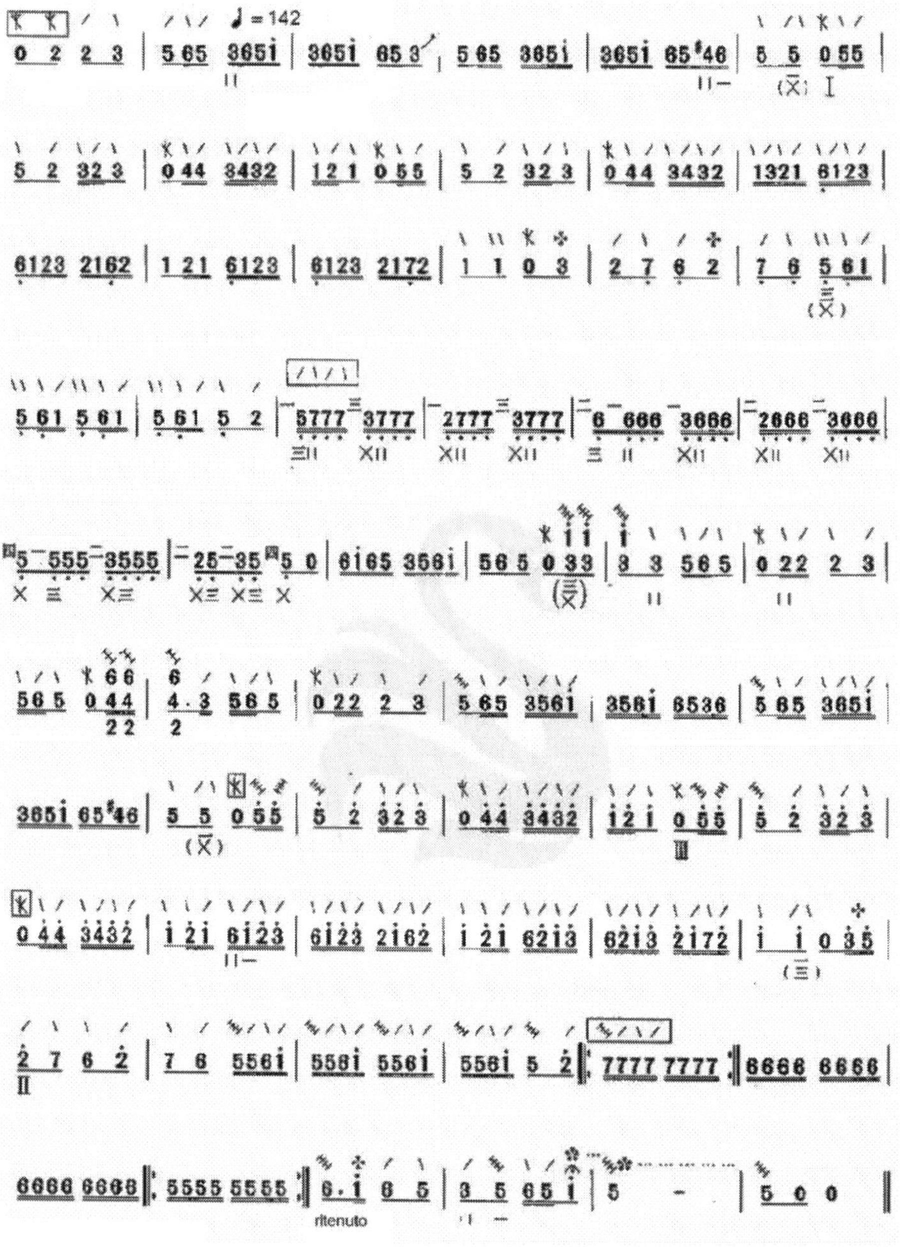
♩= 142
ritenuto

The Clouds Chasing the Moon

1 = D 4/4

Composed by Ren Guang

Adagio, con expressione

Online Materials

To know better the melodies of the above songs for practicing purposes, please refer to the YouTube videos below:

旱天雷：https://www.youtube.com/watch?v=2nF3IzfqE4A
步步高：https://www.youtube.com/watch?v=GaW7EtFfyYo
金蛇狂舞：https://www.youtube.com/watch?v=BL4Lv8TvMkc
夜深沉：https://www.youtube.com/watch?v=zcb3BPRKBFA
彩雲追月：https://www.youtube.com/watch?v=a1voDwO6K4M

Made in the USA
Coppell, TX
24 February 2021